Our Town

Kim Ulander

Contents

Rigby

A Harcourt Achieve Imprint

www.Rigby.com
1-800-531-5015

Where Do We Live?

We live in a small town.

Our town is special.

It has places to live

and places to play.

Let's take a trip around our town!

Where Do We Go to Learn?

We learn at school.

The school is on First Street.

It is near some houses.

Many children walk to school.

Can you find the school?

Our Town

School   Library   Post Office

First Street

Market

Main Street

River Road

Park

Where Do We Play?

We play at the park.

The park is on River Road.

The park has lots of hills and trees.

It has a trail around a pond.

Can you find the park?

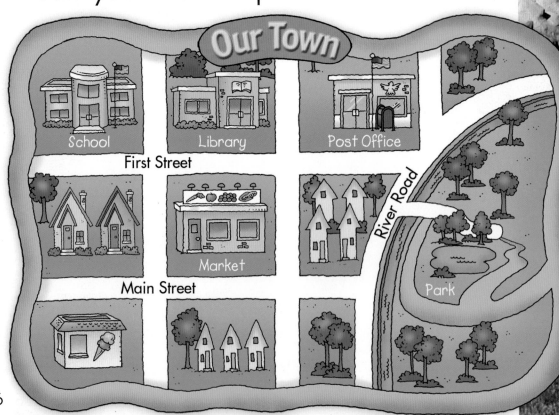

Our Town

School

Library

Post Office

First Street

Market

River Road

Main Street

Park

Where Do We Get Books?

We get books at the library.

The library is on First Street.

The library has many

different kinds of books.

Can you find the library?

Our Town

School

Library

Post Office

First Street

River Road

Market

Main Street

Park

Where Do We Get Food?

We get food at the market.

The market is on Main Street.

It has fresh fruit and

other good food, too.

Can you find the market?

Our Town

School

Library

Post Office

First Street

River Road

Market

Main Street

Park

Where Do We Mail Letters?

We mail letters at the post office.
The post office is on First Street.
You can send mail and
buy stamps there, too.
Can you find the post office?

Our Town

School Library Post Office

First Street

Market

River Road

Main Street

Park

Where Is Our Favorite Place?

Our favorite place in town
is the ice cream store.
And we are so happy!
Do you know why?
We live right by the ice cream store!

15

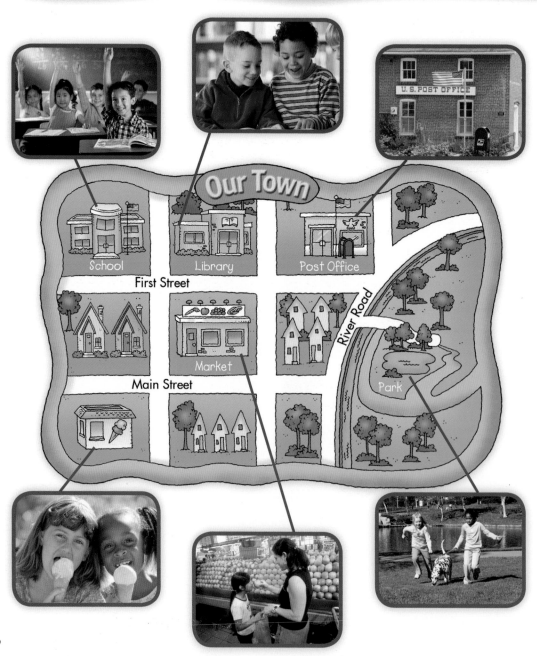

Our Town

School

Library

Post Office

First Street

River Road

Market

Main Street

Park